CELLS ARE US

Written by
Dr Fran Balkwill
Illustrated by
Mic Rolph

HarperCollins*Publishers*

First published in 1990
Reprinted 1992
© text Fran Balkwill 1990
© illustrations Mic Rolph 1990
A CIP catalogue record of this book is available from the British Library
ISBN 0 00 191163 5
ISBN 0 00 196306 6 (PB)

Printed and bound in The People's Republic of China
This book is set in Lubalin Graph 13/16

Once upon a time before you were born, two cells collided, one big, one small. The big cell (the egg) and the small cell (the sperm) became one very special cell...

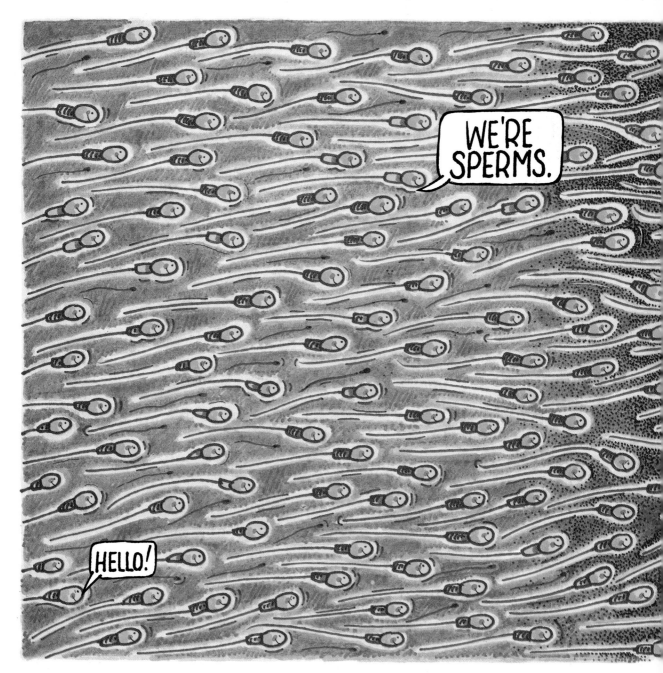

Every living creature on earth, from ants to zebras, from woodworm to whales, began life just like you as a single tiny cell.

What are cells?

Cells are the "building blocks" of life. Your body is made of zillions and zillions of them. Each one is so tiny you can't even see it with a magnifying glass.
You need a special instrument called a microscope.

When you look at cells under a microscope, using a very powerful lens, you can distinctly see hundreds of them.
With the most powerful lens you can see a single cell.

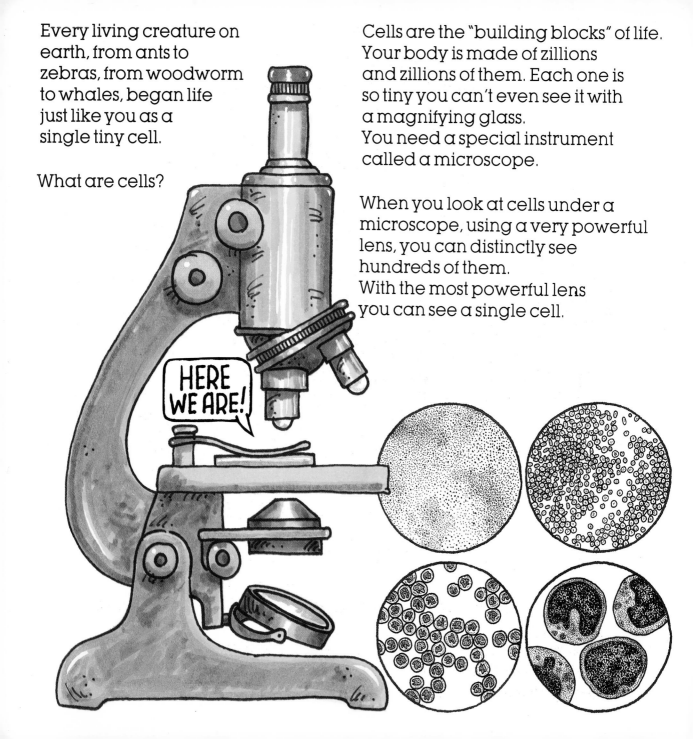

But how did you grow from just one cell?

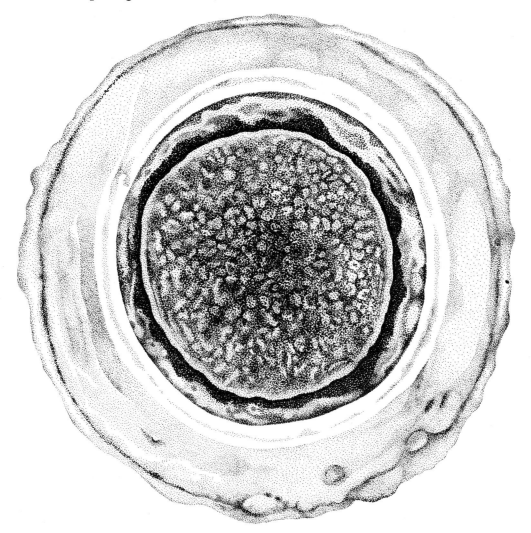

That first cell had all the information and instructions to make
you as you are now.
It was all in a secret code in the middle of the cell.
This code is called DNA. It is a very long list of instructions
that gives each cell in your body its own shape and function.

That first cell grew a little and then "wiggly" bits called chromosomes
(krome-o-soames) could clearly be seen.
Half of the chromosomes came from the egg cell and half from the
sperm cell.
The chromosomes contained two copies of that secret code,
the plans to make you.

The first cell then divided into two separate
cells, using a process called cell division
and this is how it happened . . .

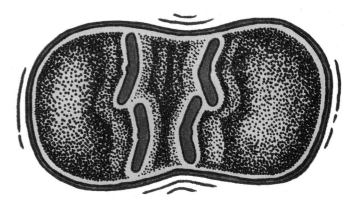

First the chromosomes lined
up in the centre of the cell.

Then each chromosome split into
two identical halves.

THWOP!

Next the cell made a fold
down its middle-

HEY PRESTO !!! -Two cells, which both
had all the information and instructions
to make you . . . and then . . .

9

Those 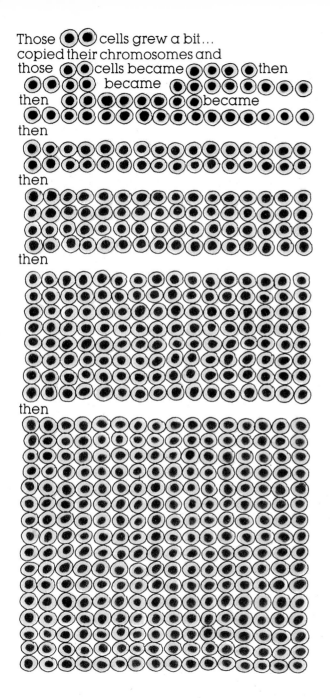 cells grew a bit…
copied their chromosomes and
those cells became then
became then
then became
then

then

then

then

then

then

Very soon there were

MILLIONS

Millions of cells that now began to look different from each other . . .

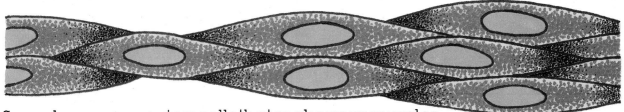

Some became cells that make your skin.

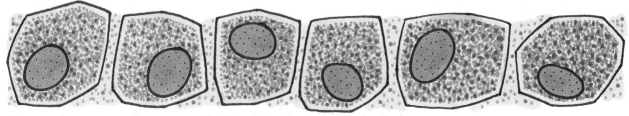

Some became moving cells that make your muscles.

Some became bone cells that make your skeleton.

Some became blood cells that carry oxygen around your body.

Some became nerve cells that relay messages. And many many more. In fact there are over 200 different cell types in your body.

But your cells didn't really grow in straight lines.
They grew in a ball shape like this.

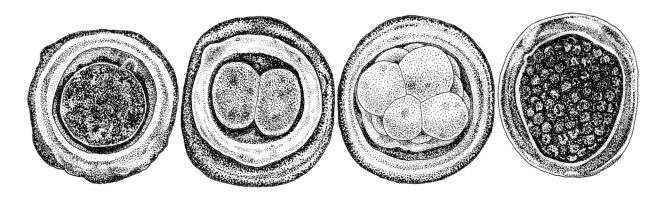

Still doesn't look much like **You** does it?

As your cells began
to make more and
more cells the ball
began to change
shape.
So now you had a
head, tiny arms,
legs, and a tail!
Yes, you once had
a tail.
At this stage it
looks as if you were
going to turn
into a fish.

·You didn't, did you?

Your cells carried on growing and dividing
so that by 40 weeks (9 months), or thereabouts,
that very first cell had divided into millions and millions
of cells doing all kinds of different, difficult and
amazing jobs, so that when you
were born you could

Of course you didn't stop there, you carried on growing because your
cells kept on dividing and you haven't stopped growing yet.

So now it's time to be introduced to some of your cells and find out about the jobs they do. But remember . . . cells are so tiny that you could fit a hundred or more on the full stop at the end of this sentence.

If one of your cells was really this size you'd be as tall as the Empire State Building in America.

(1cm)

TOOT!

Let's start on the outside of your body. Skin cells have the important job of protecting your inside and outside from extremes of cold and heat, from sharp and sticky objects, from wind, rain, and everyday dirt.

They make a layer about ten living cells deep and they keep it that way by replacing themselves regularly.

As they get older and higher up the layer, they become tougher and tougher, scalier and scalier, until they die and float off into the atmosphere to form dust.

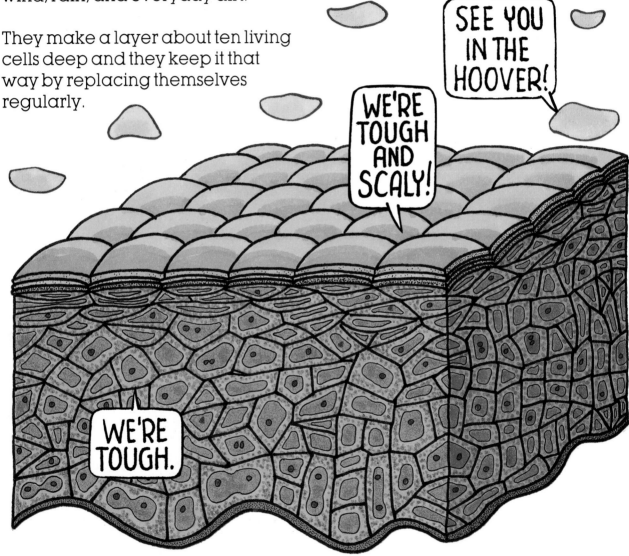

Some parts of your skin need to be tougher than others, so the dead cell layer gets thicker to protect you – the skin on your heel feels tougher than the skin on your face, doesn't it?

Did you know that millions of skin cells float off your body every day? Give your leg a quick scratch . . . You've just got rid of a few hundred thousand of them.

Skin cells also give your body its colour.
It doesn't matter who you are.

Everybody's skin cells are all exactly the same, except that they make
different amounts of special colouring substances
called melanin and carotene.
If your skin is pale and you go to a hot country
for a holiday, your cells make more melanin
to protect you.
But be VERY careful, too much sun can make
you ill.

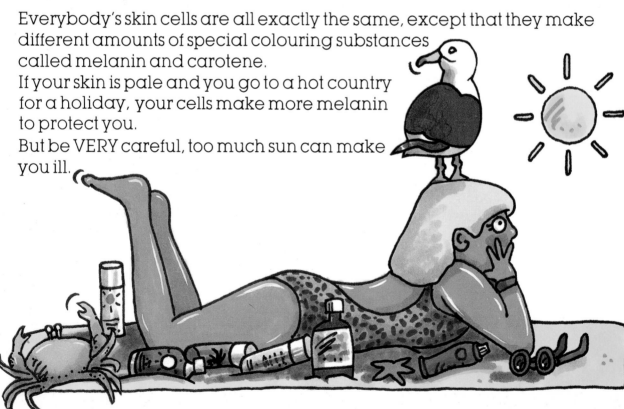

Now we'll go inside your body.
All your cells need food to grow and
divide. Blood carries liquid food
around your body, into every nook
and cranny.

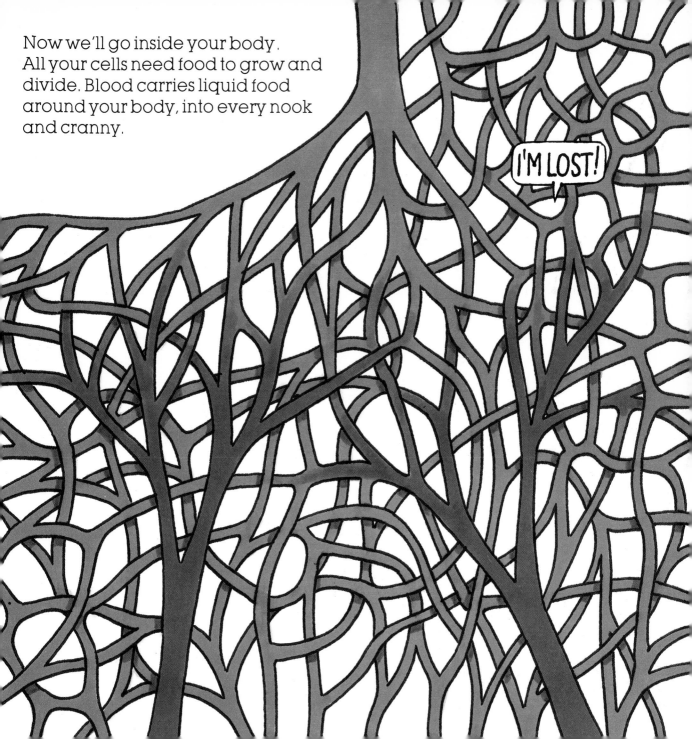

Blood flows in big tubes called arteries
(art-er-ees), that branch and branch until they
almost disappear into little tubes called
capillaries (cap-ill-a-rees). Then the
capillaries become bigger again and
join up to form big tubes called veins
which go to the heart.

Blood is liquid isn't it?
But what does that liquid contain?
You've guessed it (if you haven't just pretend).
Yes . . . cells.

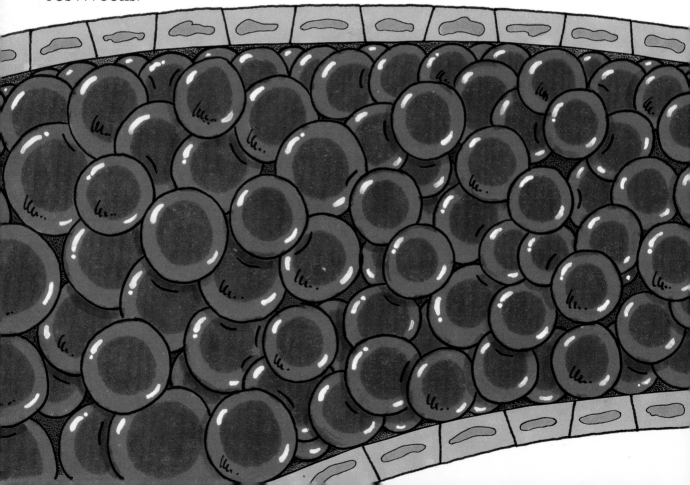

Blood is always red because it contains
zillions of red cells.
Did you know that your body has to make about one
hundred and fifty million blood cells every minute of
your life to replace ones that die?

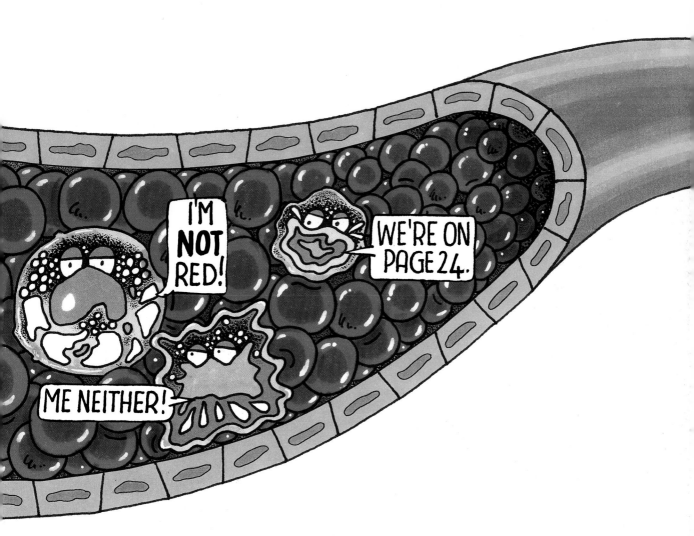

The red cells in your blood have a vital job to do. They carry an important gas called oxygen (ox-ejen) around your body. Without oxygen all your cells would die. The air that you breathe into your lungs contains oxygen.

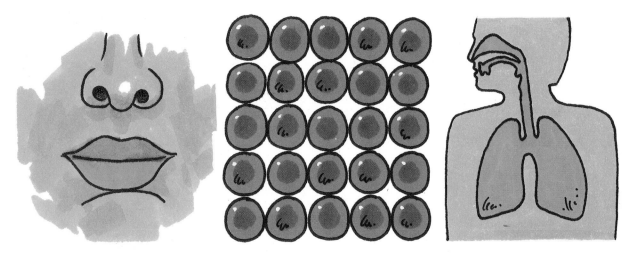

Deep breath! Haemoglobin (Heem-o-glo-bin), a special substance inside red blood cells, picks up oxygen from your lung cells,

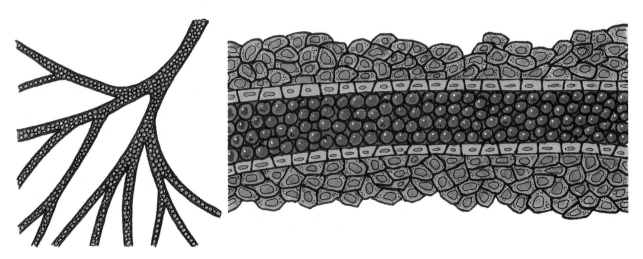

takes it through the arteries and capillaries of the blood stream and releases it to cells that need it. When each breath of oxygen has been used up,

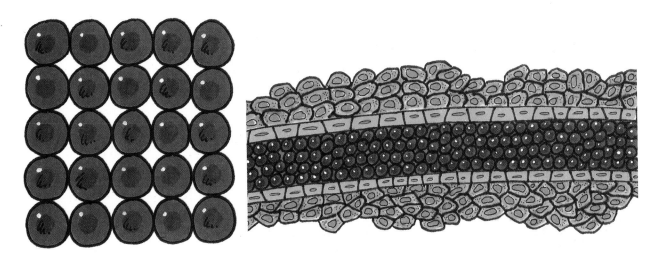

another gas, not a nice one, called carbon dioxide (carbon di-ox-ide) remains. It makes the red blood cells a bit blue.

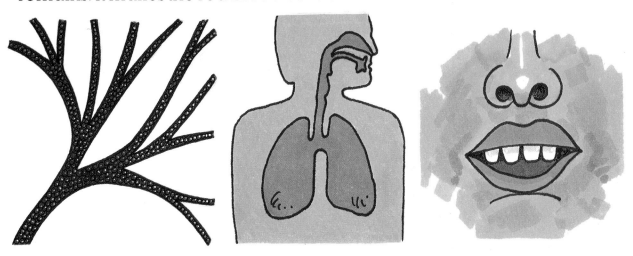

Red blood cells carry the carbon dioxide back through the capillaries and veins to the lungs. Breathe out!

There are some other very special blood cells,
neutrophils (new-tro-fils), macrophages (mac-ro-fay-jes)
and lymphocytes (lim-fo-sites),

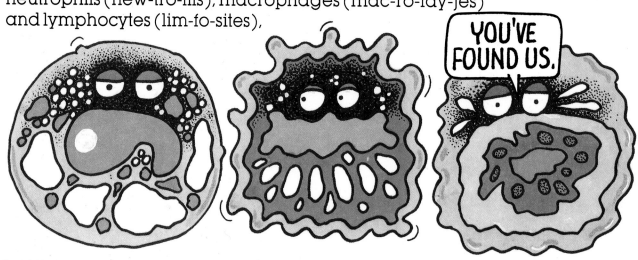

but they are not red, they are white. They are your defender cells.

Their job is to constantly patrol the blood stream, fighting off all the nasty
viruses and bacteria that make you ill.

If they don't destroy the bad germs when they meet them, they send out messages for reinforcements, and millions more white cells join in.

So when you've got measles, or wheezles, or sneezles, remember your white blood cells working away to make you better.

Do you imagine that
cells are rather
squidgy things?
What do you think
your bones are
made of?
Surely bones aren't
made of cells —
surprisingly,
they are!

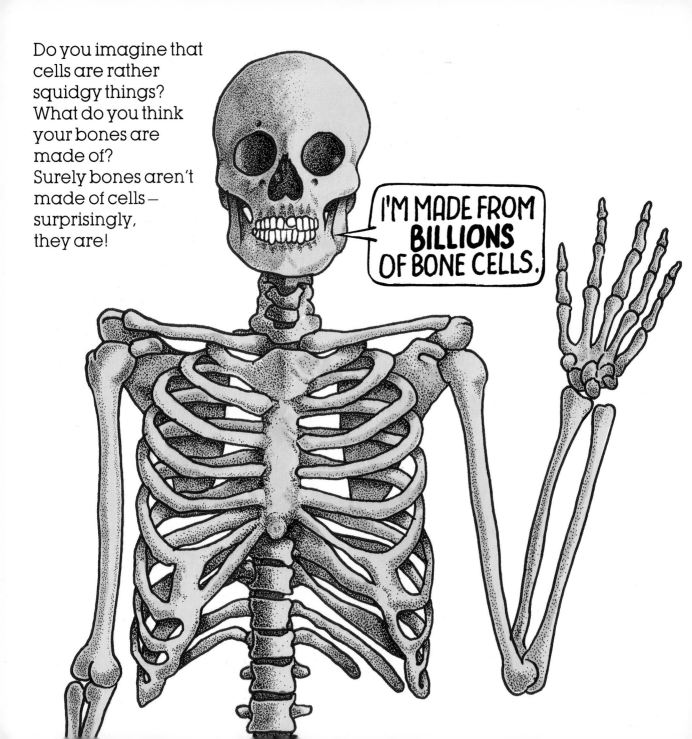

But how do bone cells make your skeleton? Well, each bone cell is like a factory churning out really tough stuff which surrounds the cells and sets hard.

Bone cells make 206 bones in your body. Without them, you'd be a squelchy mess on the floor!

I FEEL SPLUDGY!

Muscle cells are long, thin, S-T-R-E-T-C-H-Y cells that make every part of your body move.

Each cell contains minute strands of elastic substances (actin and my-o-sin) that can make it shorter and fatter.

Muscle cells are tightly joined together so that they all change shape at the same time.

Nerve cells are excitable cells that send messages around your body by tiny electrical impulses.

These messages travel along thread-like parts of nerve cells called axons that run in a cord up and down your backbone.

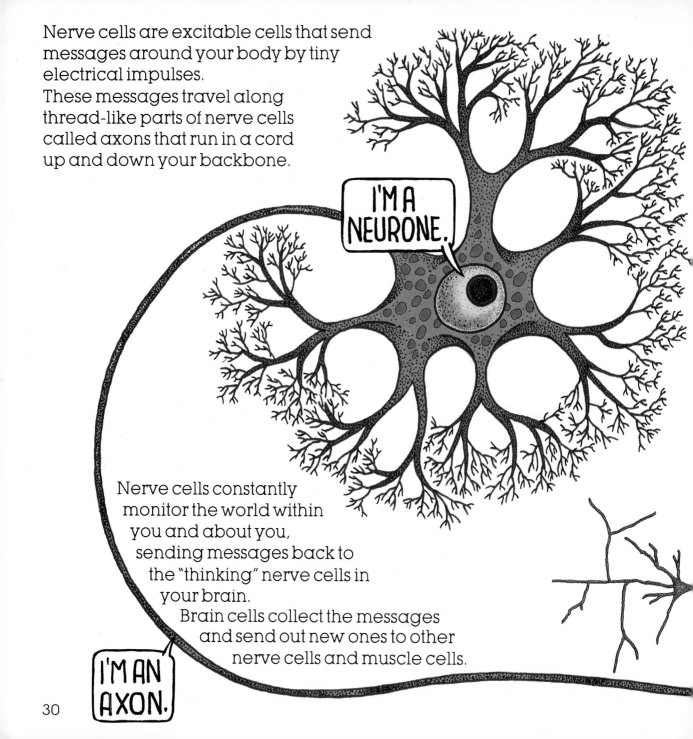

Nerve cells constantly monitor the world within you and about you, sending messages back to the "thinking" nerve cells in your brain.

Brain cells collect the messages and send out new ones to other nerve cells and muscle cells.

Some nerve cells in your brain keep parts of your body working without your thinking about it, even when you are fast asleep.

You don't have to remember to breathe or make your heart beat, do you?

Nerve cells come in some surprising shapes and sizes. One type of nerve cell that controls your leg and arm muscles is the same width as other cells in your body, but can be up to one metre long!

There are, of course, many other cells in your body.
For instance, cells that work your stomach, lungs, liver,
kidneys, cells that make your teeth, nails and hair.
Scientists all over the world have learnt a lot about
your amazing body – but they don't know the
whole story.
As scientists learn more about cells, they should find
new cures for diseases such as cancer and AIDS.

The exciting challenge for future scientists (maybe you?)
is to understand completely how a hundred
million million cells work together in harmony,
to make you grow and keep you healthy, and how
they all developed in such a precise and intricate
pattern, from that first tiny cell . . . that was you.

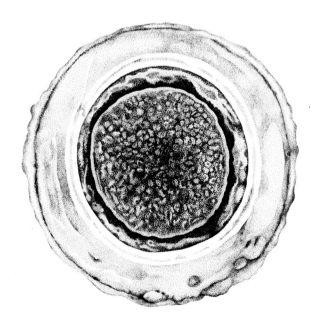